… I CAN READ ABOUT

INDIANS

Written by Elizabeth Warren

Illustrated by Virginia McWilliams

Troll Associates

Copyright © 1975 by Troll Associates
All rights reserved. No part of this book may be used or reproduced
in any manner whatsoever without written permission from the publisher.
Printed in the United States of America. Troll Associates, Mahwah, N.J.
Library of Congress Catalog Card Number: 74-24880

Long, long ago, Indians came to live in America.

They came across the snowbound north, from Siberia to Alaska. Some settled in Canada. Some travelled to what is now the United States. Others went as far as South America.

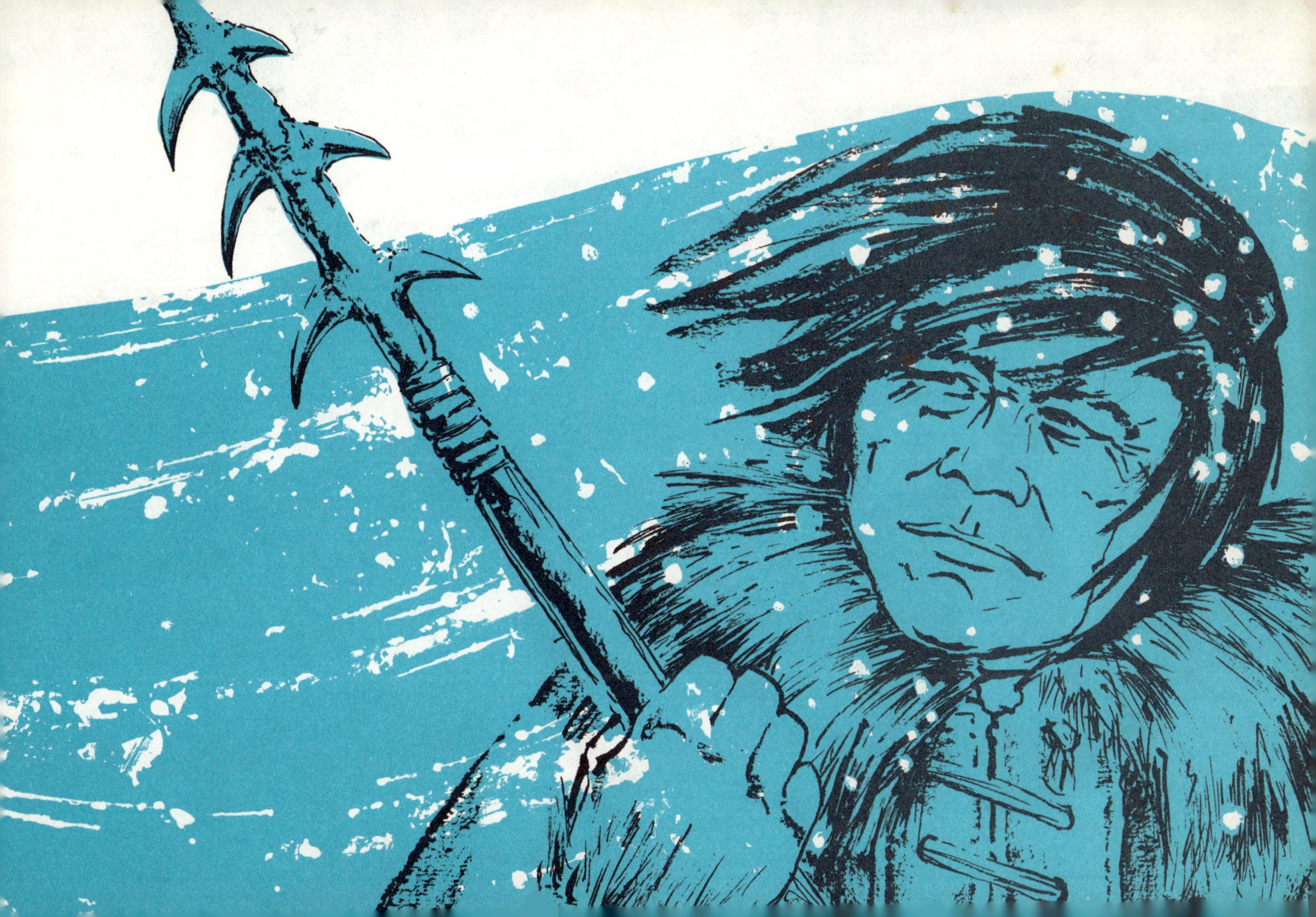

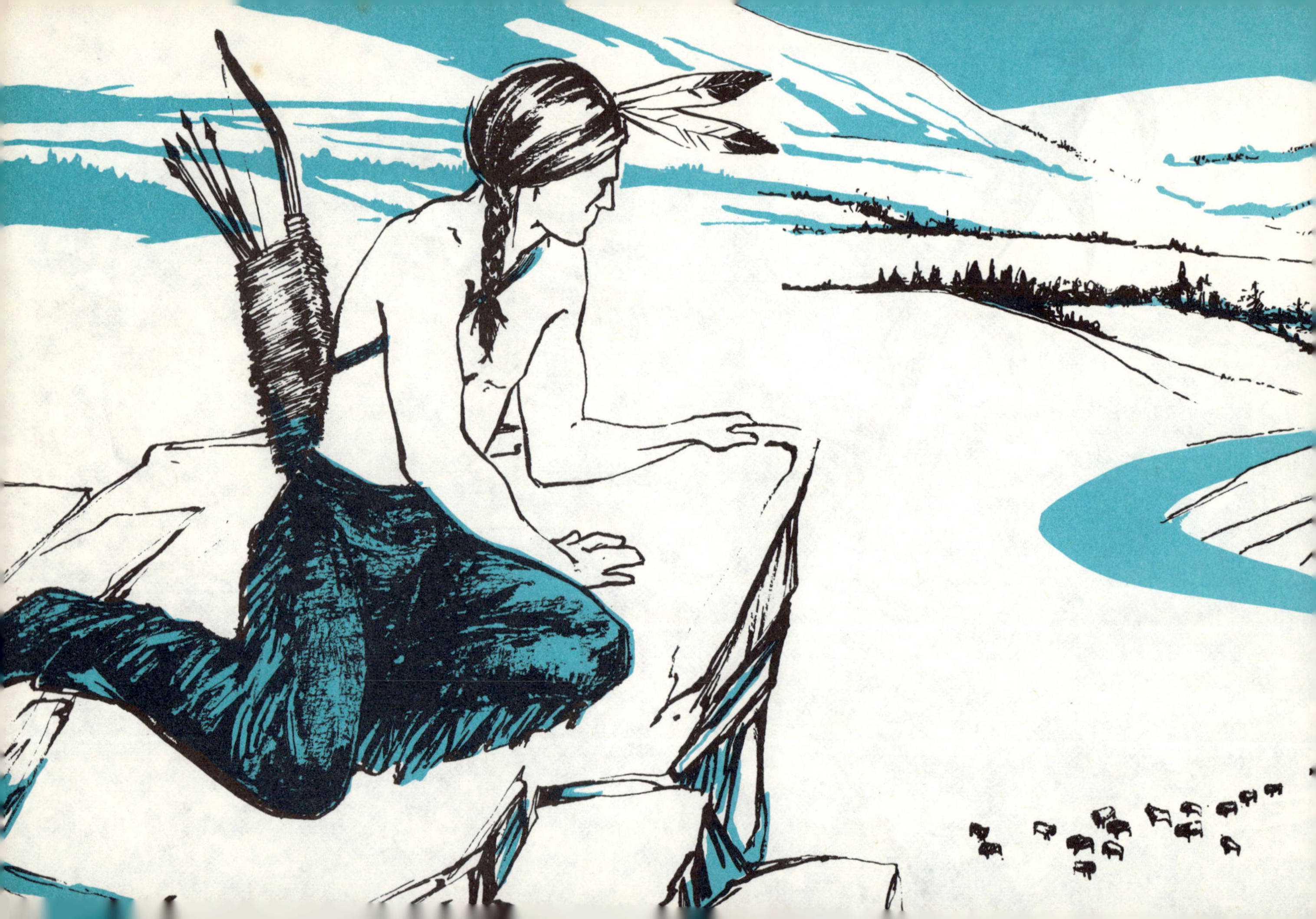

When the Indians came to America, they found a land filled with mountains and prairies, rivers and streams. They found green forests, and blue lakes bursting with fish. Animals roamed the earth and birds filled the air.

Thousands of years later, a man named Columbus made a big mistake. He was looking for India but landed in America.

When the people came to meet him, he mistakenly called them Indians. But they were not Indians. They were the first Americans.

In their search for food and shelter, the Indians of America moved across the country and settled in different places.

They settled in groups called tribes. Some tribes chose the woodlands for their home. They had names like Shawnee, Chippewa, and Kickapoo.

The houses they built were called wigwams. They were made of poles that were bent and covered with the bark of trees. In the middle of each wigwam, a fire burned to keep the family warm.

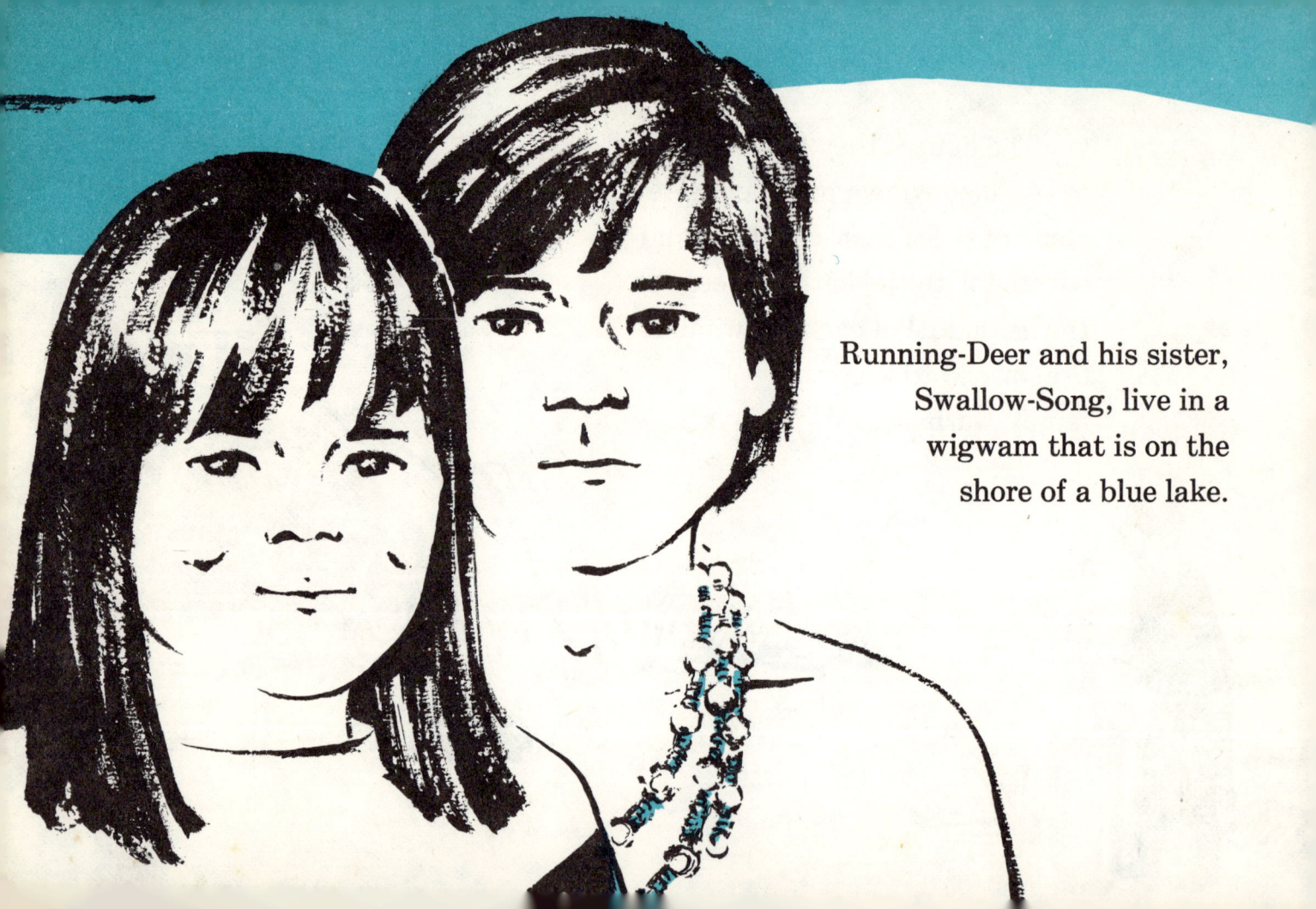

Running-Deer and his sister, Swallow-Song, live in a wigwam that is on the shore of a blue lake.

Behind their house is a
garden, and behind their garden
the forest grows.

Gray-Wolf, their father, made his canoe out of birch bark.

He uses it to travel, and to harvest the wild rice that grows along the lake shore.

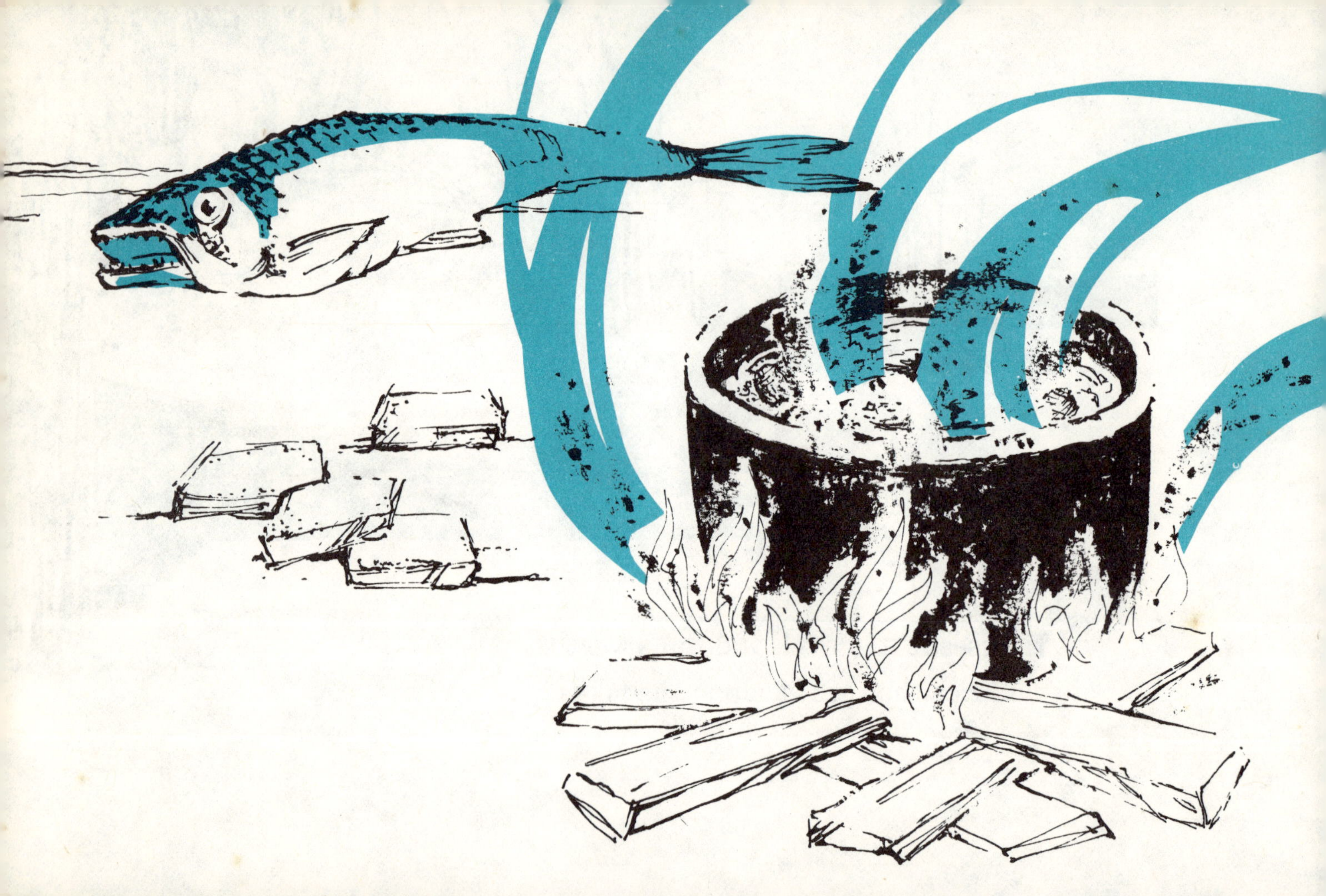

Today, he has brought home a fish for the noon meal.
There will be stewed pumpkin and succotash from the garden.
The children's mother, White-Doe, has baked bread and
crisp little corn cakes. There will be tea and wild blueberries.
How good it is when the food is plentiful!

A shortage of food is a serious matter. When there is a problem, the tribe gathers in a circle around a large fire and has a powwow. They discuss their needs. Sometimes a medicine man, or shaman, offers prayers to the spirits. Drums beat and rattles shake. The Indians dance and sing.

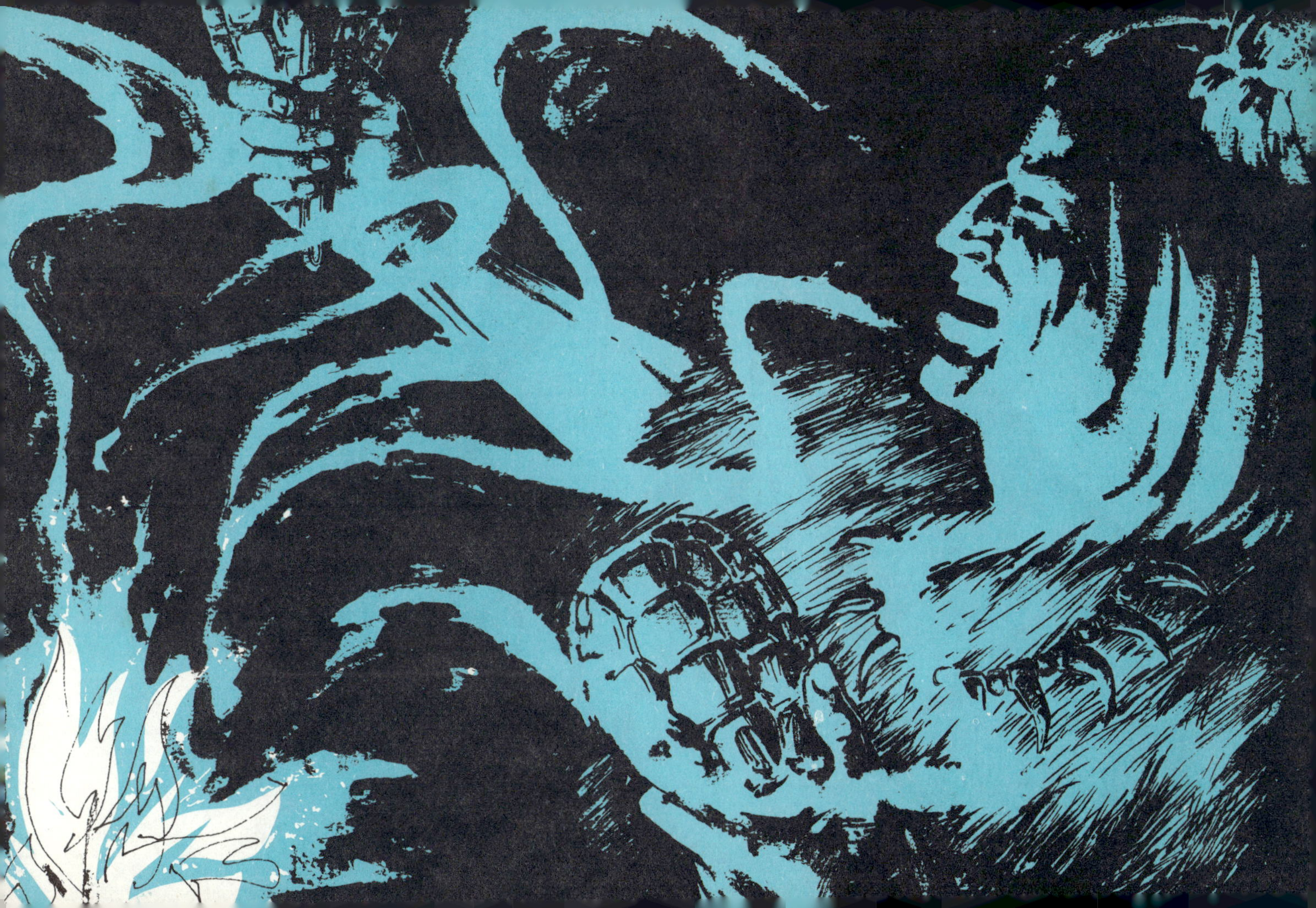

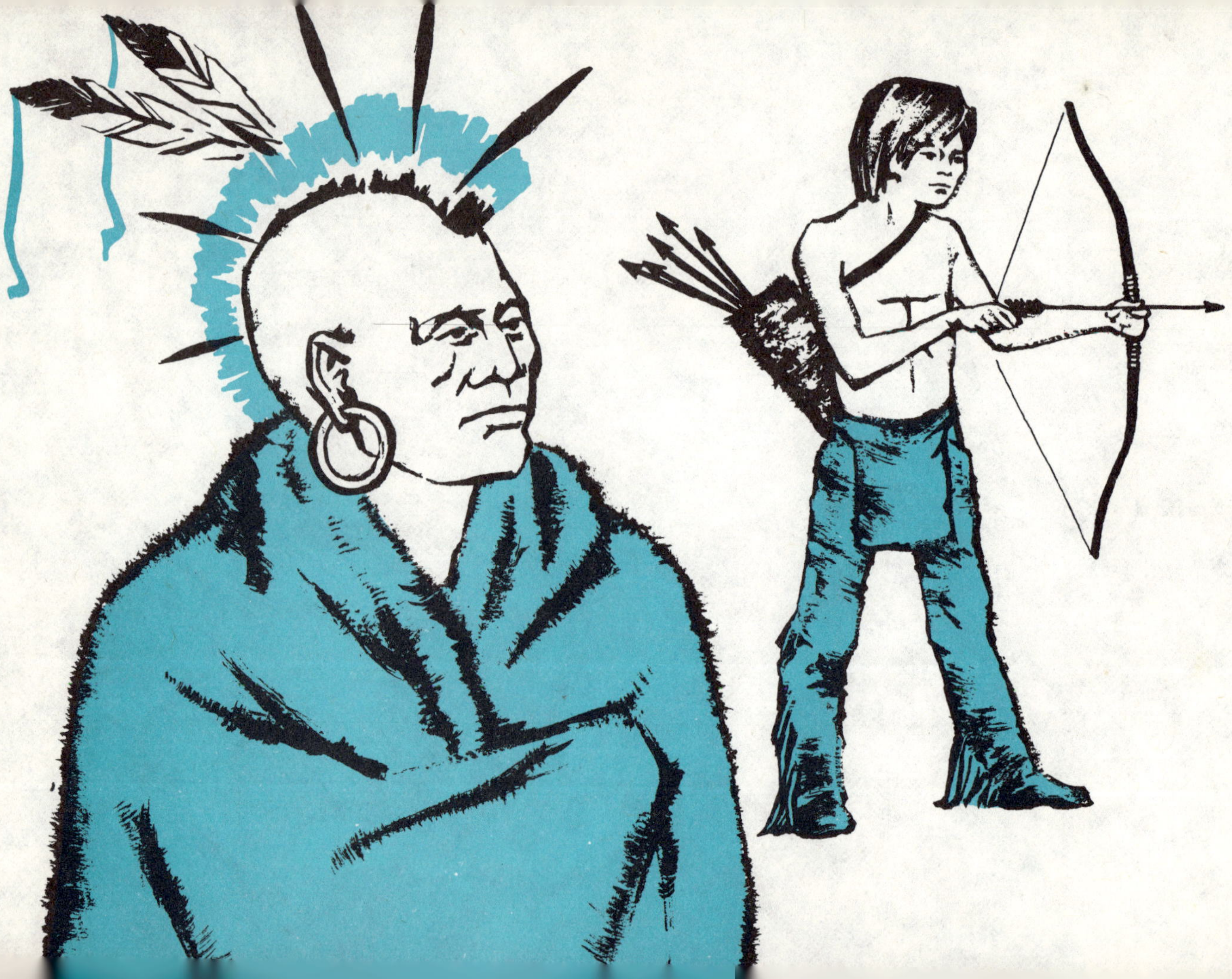

In fine weather, Gray-Wolf and Running-Deer go hunting in the forest.

Gray-Wolf is teaching his son to hunt and trap. He is teaching him how to use a bow and arrow and how to throw a tomahawk so that it will split a twig at twenty paces.

Running-Deer must learn how to be a brave warrior and hunter.

At first, Running-Deer is clumsy. His arrows miss the target many times. But Gray-Wolf is patient and Running-Deer learns. Soon he will be good enough to hunt big game with the men of his tribe. Moose, elk, deer . . . maybe even a bear!

Animals are very important to the Indians. Their meat provides food for the tribe. Their hides are hung from tall poles to dry, and the skins are tanned and used to make leggings and moccasins. The fur is sewn into soft, warm blankets. Even bones and antlers are used. They are turned into tools and arrowheads.

After Gray-Wolf hunts, he ties the tail of the animal to a twig, and offers thanks to the dead animal's spirit. Gray-Wolf has a great respect for life and takes only what he needs.

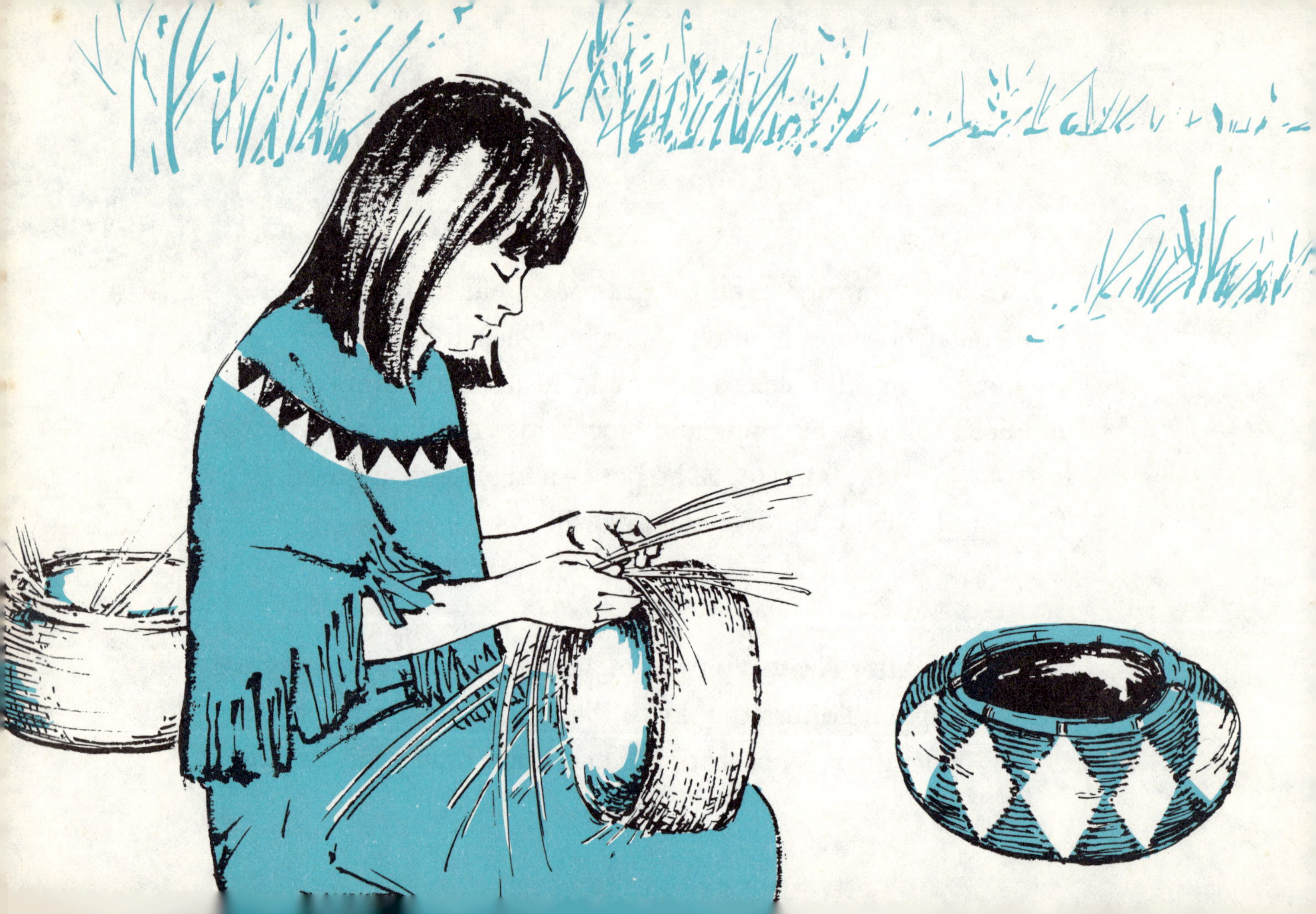

There are many things for a young Indian girl to do.
Swallow-Song learns to tie the knots for the fish nets.
She weaves baskets and mats from grass and rushes. Her
mother has taught her how to make cooking pots from clay.
It is her job to watch the fire outside their home. Each
day she sweeps the hearth with a grass broom and sprinkles
it with water.

She helps her mother make moccasins lined with rabbit fur to keep them warm in winter.

With the other village women, they sit in the sun and sew. Their needles are made from animal bones or porcupine quills. And, because they are Indians of the forests, the designs they sew and paint on their clothing are of the forests, too. They are designs of leaves and vines and flowers.

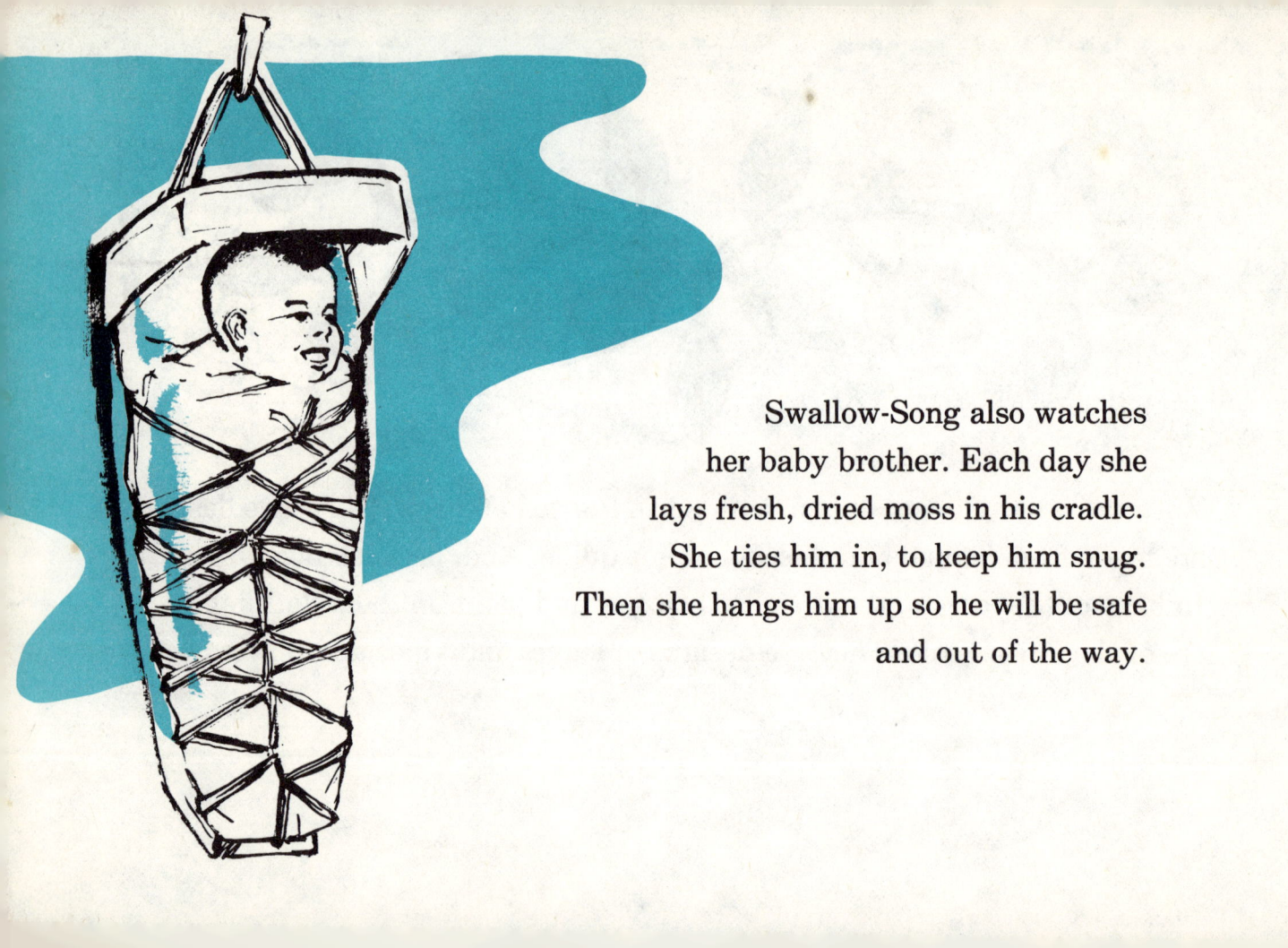

Swallow-Song also watches her baby brother. Each day she lays fresh, dried moss in his cradle. She ties him in, to keep him snug. Then she hangs him up so he will be safe and out of the way.

Sometimes she straps the cradle board to her back. That way he can keep her company and she can sing softly to him about the sun and the moon and the stars, and about little squirrels asleep in the trees.

But not all Indians settled in the woodlands and forests. Some settled on the open prairies. They had no deep woods, only the flat plains sweeping in every direction. They had names like Blackfoot, Cheyenne, and Pawnee.

Some lived in lodges made of wood, which were covered with grass and earth. Shaped like a circle, the insides of these lodges were usually 20 to 60 feet across. In every lodge a fire burned, and curls of smoke rose in the air from openings in the roofs.

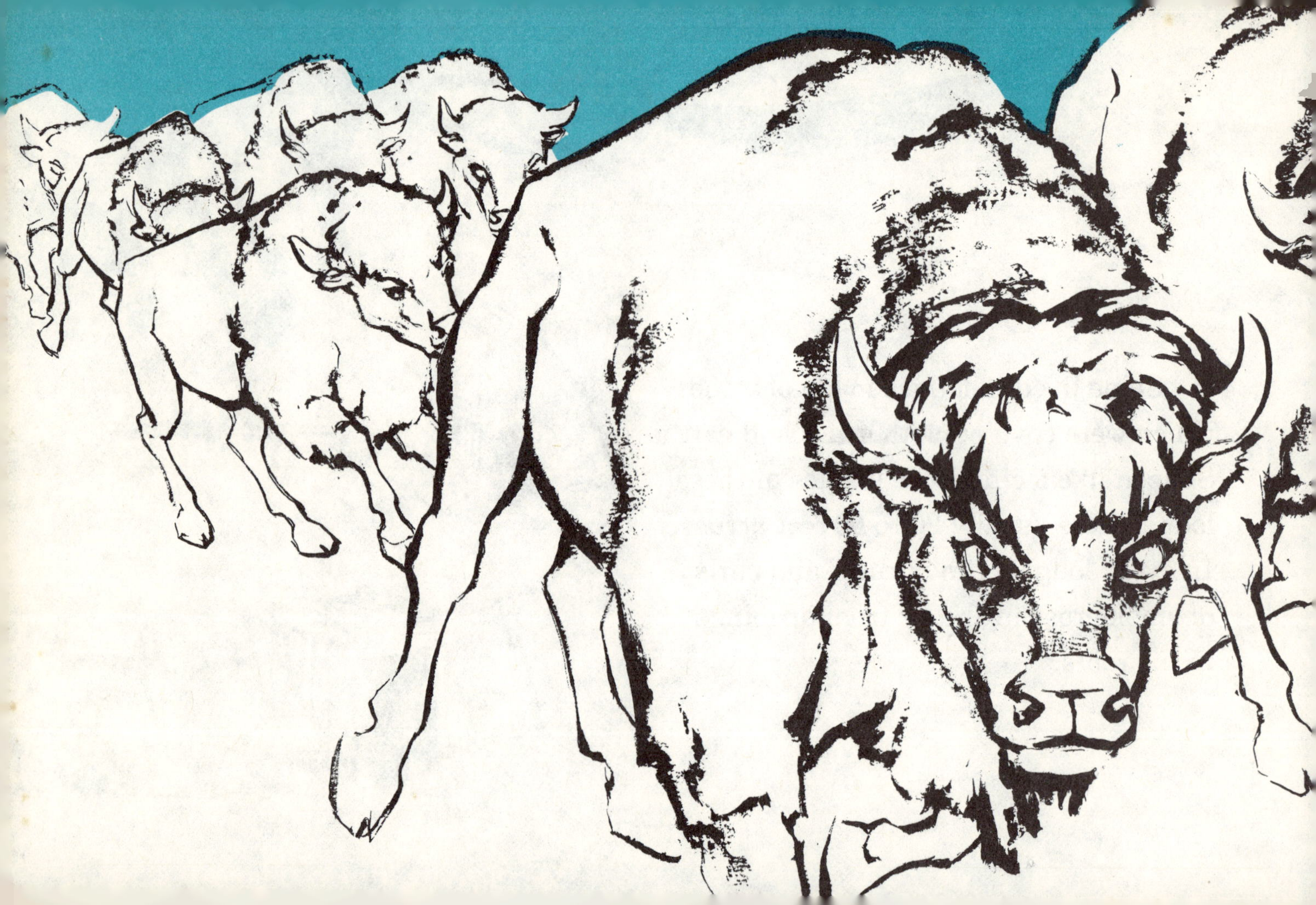

Great bison roamed the prairies at that time.
When they galloped, they sounded like thunder from the earth.
Indians of the Plains needed them for food, shelter and clothing.

Indians who hunted the roaming herds of bison often lived in tents called teepees. Teepees could be taken down, moved, and set up again without much difficulty.

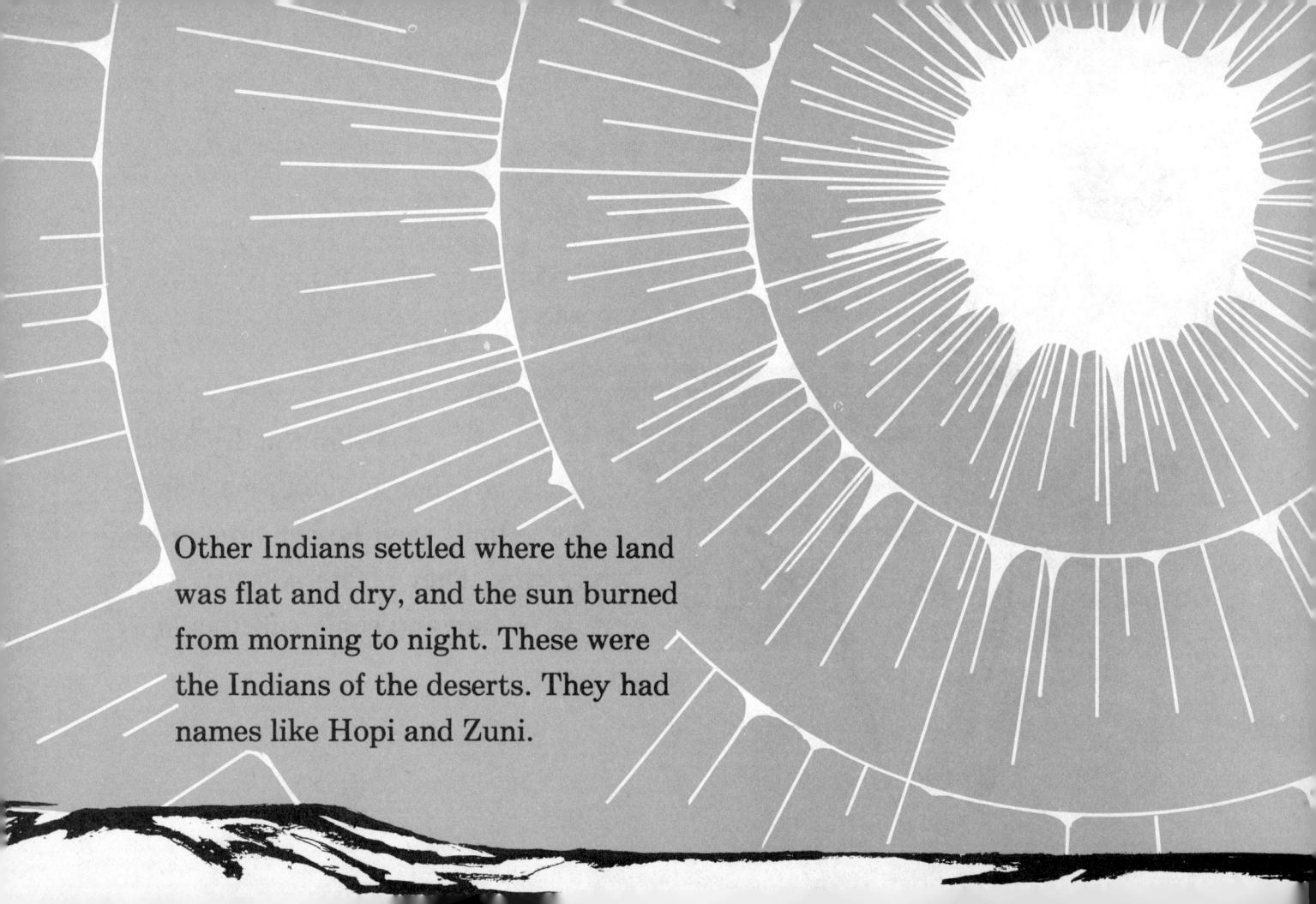

Other Indians settled where the land was flat and dry, and the sun burned from morning to night. These were the Indians of the deserts. They had names like Hopi and Zuni.

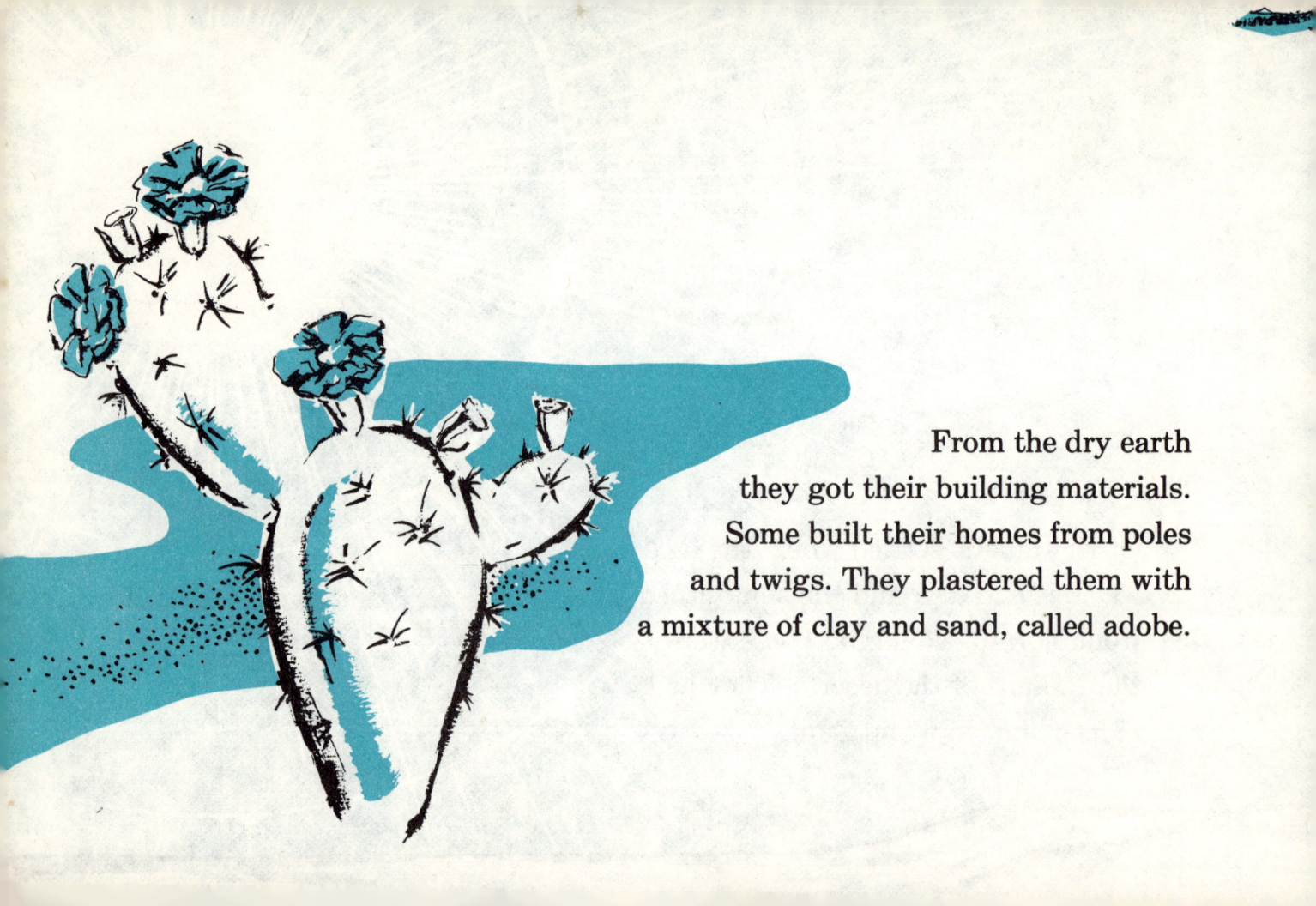

From the dry earth
they got their building materials.
Some built their homes from poles
and twigs. They plastered them with
a mixture of clay and sand, called adobe.

When the Spanish explorers came to this land, they called these Indian villages "pueblos." Pueblo is the Spanish name for *village*. And the people of these villages are still called Pueblo Indians.

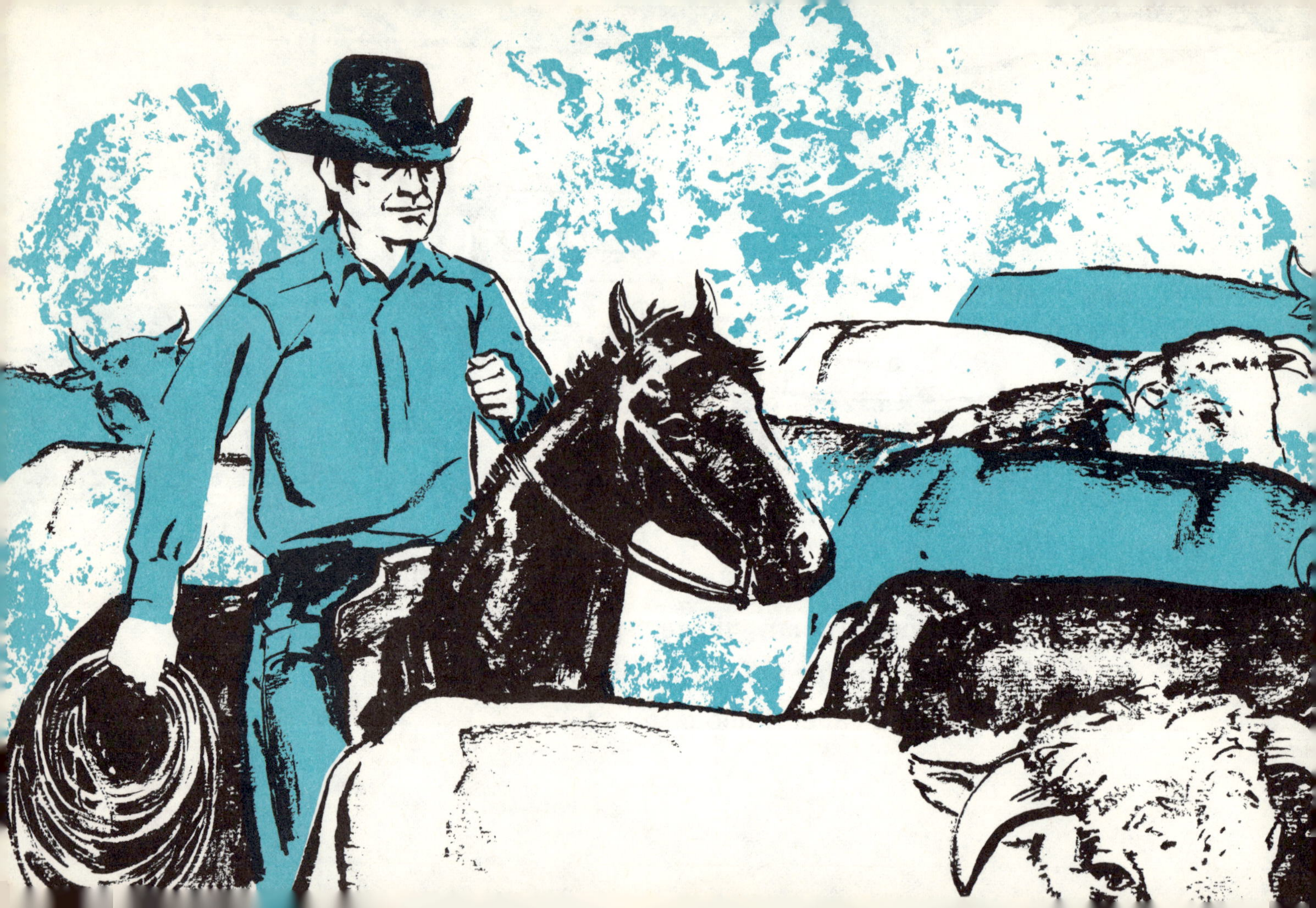

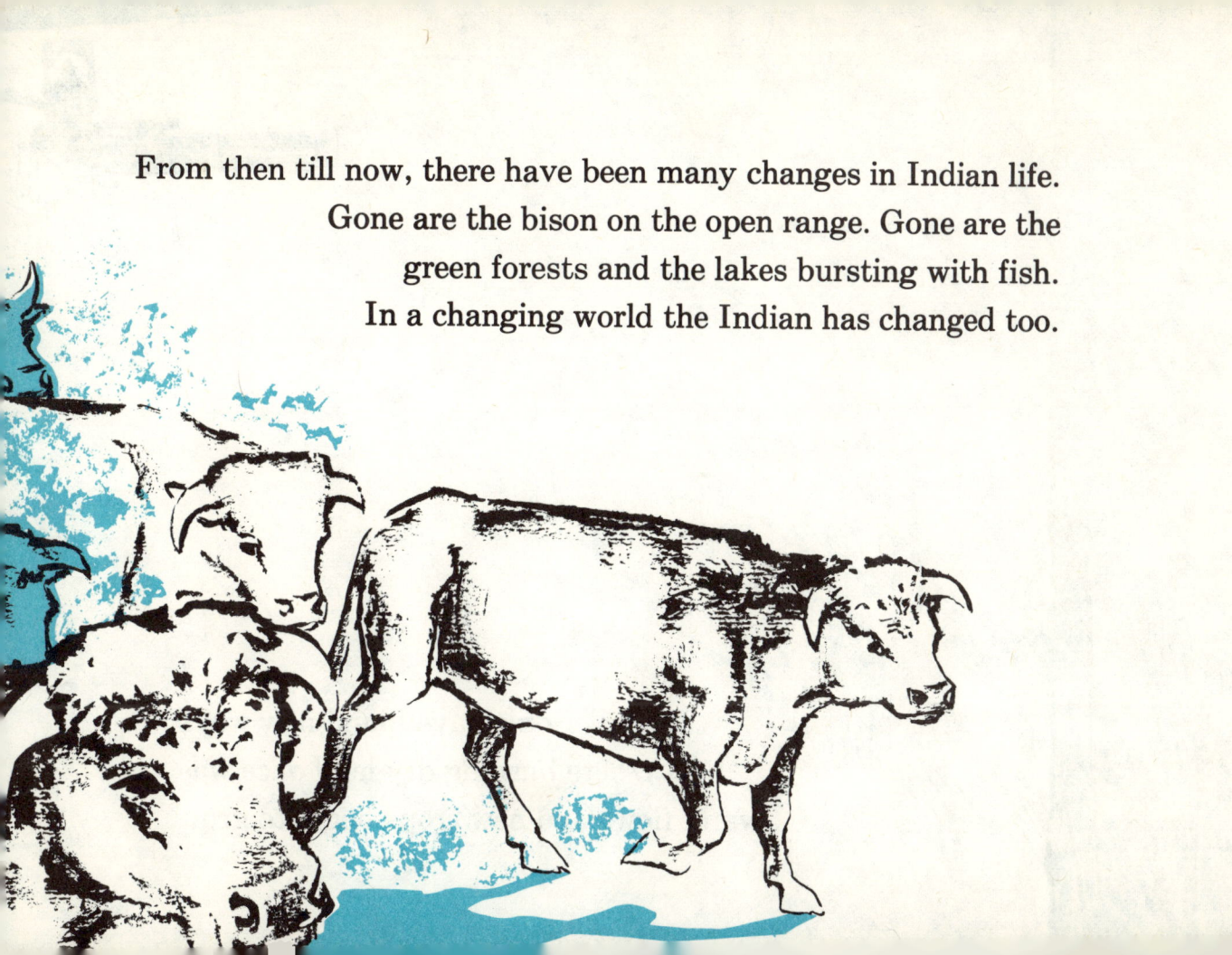

From then till now, there have been many changes in Indian life.
Gone are the bison on the open range. Gone are the
green forests and the lakes bursting with fish.
In a changing world the Indian has changed too.

Some have found new ways.
Where burning dry land once was,
water flows and new crops begin to grow.

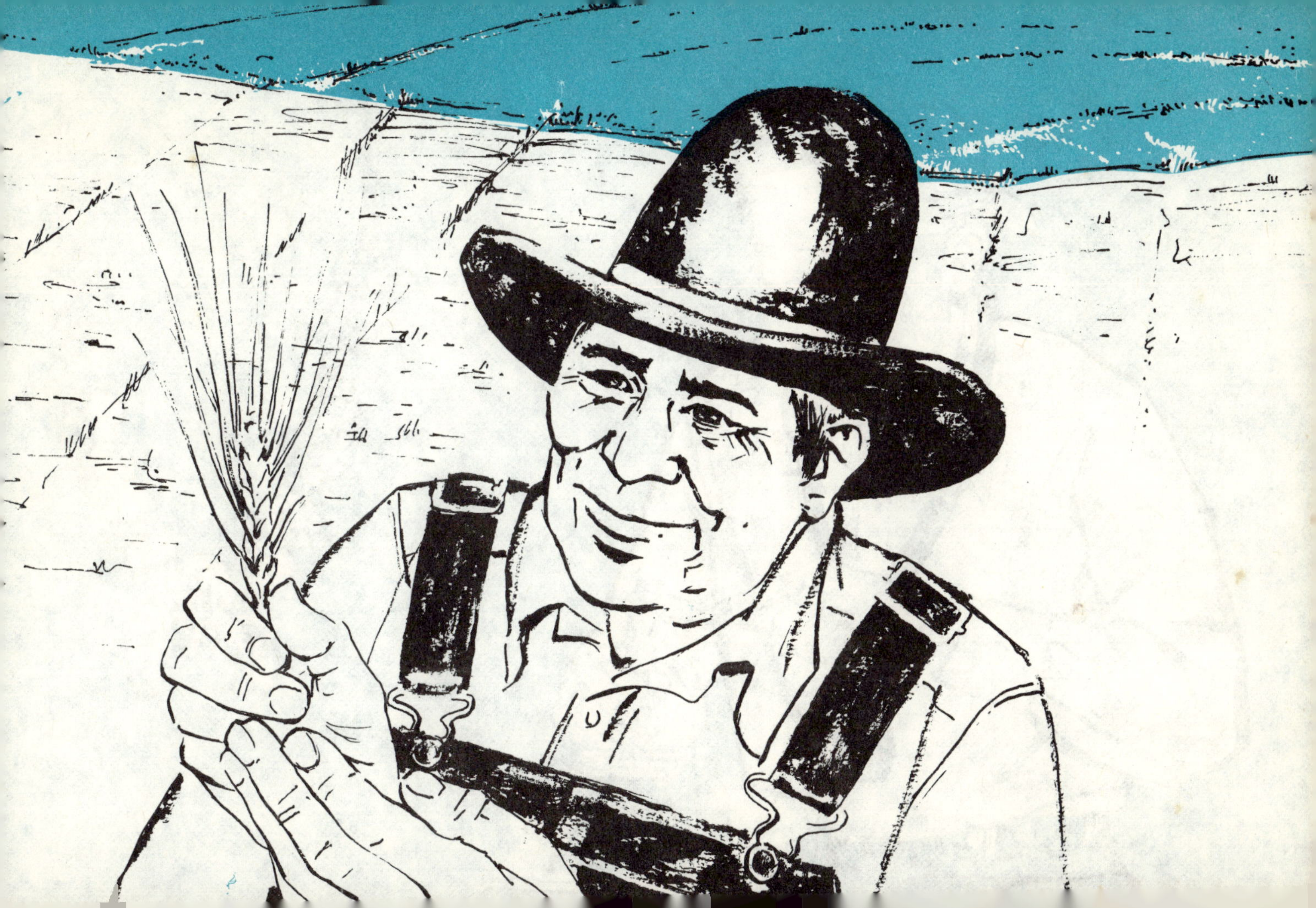

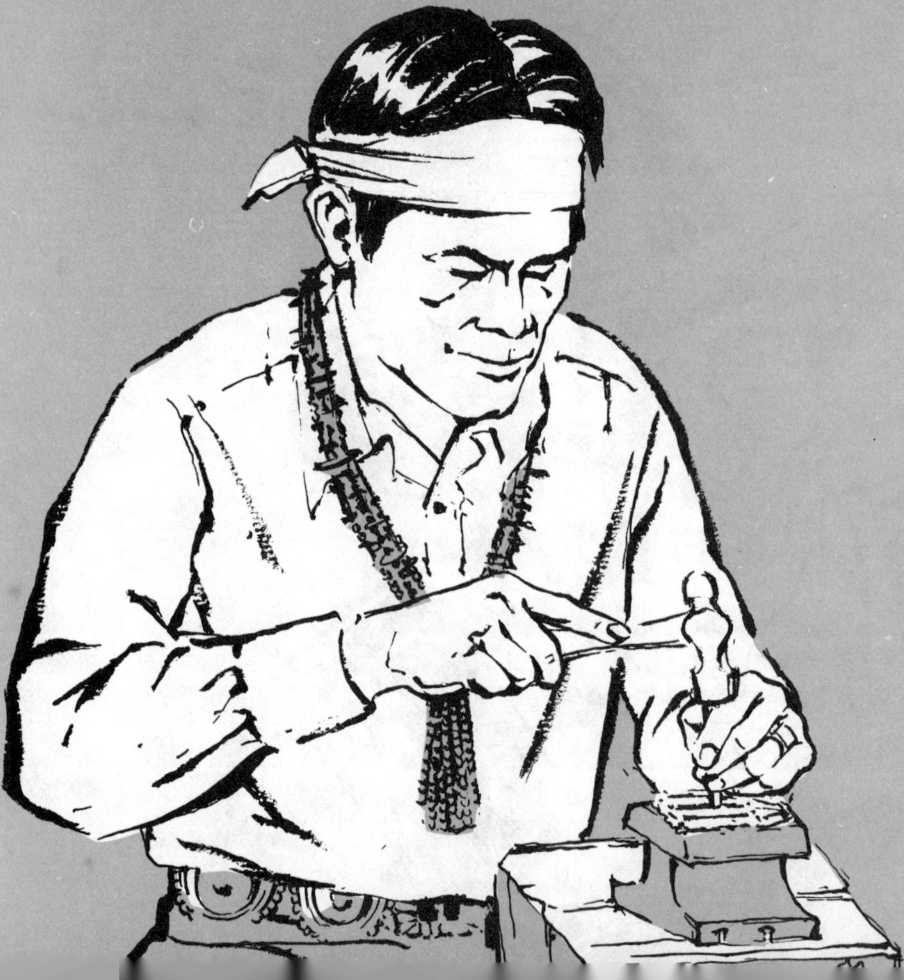

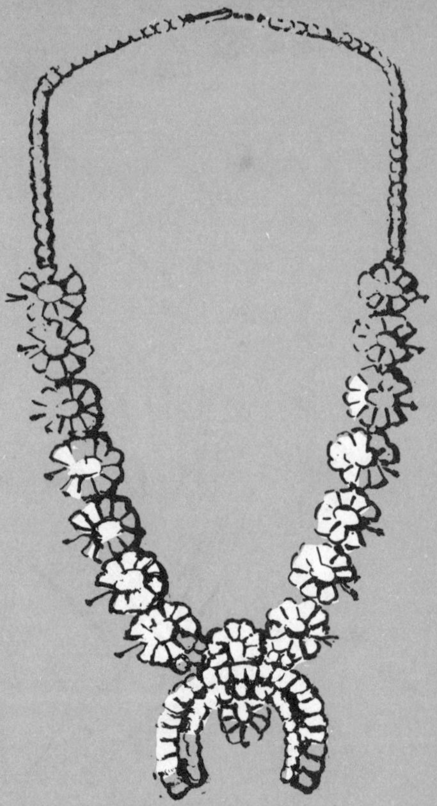

Some remember the old traditions and use them in new ways.
Craftsmen hammer and weave and sew and paint to bring
new life to forgotten beauty.

APACHES
CHEROKEES
HAVASUPAIS

In school, Indian children learn more about
their changing world. How to live in the new world . . .

... how to remember the spirit of the old.